The View from Down Here is Just Fine

Clay Dyer on Life, No Limbs, and Fishing.

What others are saying about
The View from Down Here is Just Fine:

Clay Dyer is an inspiration to all of us, a one-in-a-million guy that was put here for the rest of us to learn from. Only Scot Laney could write this story. Laney has a knack for choosing words as if in limited supply, a master at the art of concise story telling that relates well to readers of all ages.

Jay Kumar
Founder
BassFan.com
Co-host ESPN's Loud Mouth Bass

This is the story of a young man that has a passion unsurpassed in fishing. Clay is simply the most remarkable person I have ever met, period. Scot Laney has entertained us for years with his nine sentence opinion columns that can skewer or praise an entire industry.

Terry Brown
President
Get Outside Media
Bass fishing radio and television personality

Lucky Forward Press publications are available at special quantity discounts for bulk purchases for sales promotions, premiums, fund raising or educational use. Special books or book excerpts can also be created to fit specific needs.

For details contact:
Lucky Forward Press
Special Markets
5801 NW Cornelius Pass Road
Hillsboro, OR. 97124

(503) 597-7030 M-F 8-5 Pacific time.

As told by Scot Laney

The View from Down Here is Just Fine

Clay Dyer on Life, No Limbs, and Fishing.

The View from Down Here is Just Fine is an original publication of SMG Outdoors. This work has never before appeared in book form.

Lucky Forward Press
5801 NW Cornelius Pass Road
Hillsboro, OR. 97124

ISBN 978-0-578-01237-7
Second Lucky Forward Press Printing: June 2008

Printed in the USA

Table of Contents

Quotes From Clay

To

Clay

…and anyone else that dares to think not only outside the box but outside of the whole box factory.

Author's Notes

Clay Dyer is a one-in-a-million person, and you won't ever meet another like him. I think the mold was probably broken within only a few minutes after it was used to make him. God has a sense of humor. If you don't believe so, take the time to tell Him your plans; see how that works out. But the world is simply not ready for too many Clay Dyers, because how could the rest of us carry on with our complaints, bothers and senses of slight surrounded by a pack of Clays?

We couldn't.

So that's why Clay is a limited issue. He's an artist's proof, if you will. He's here to remind all of us sad sacks what it is that is really important, to show us that a positive attitude trumps a negative one, that perseverance can carry the day and that we all have choices to make in both of these areas.

Clay doesn't see it that way. He simply just does what he does, and it's there for us to learn from or not, our choice. He'll share with you why it is he does what he does, and even how he does it, if you ask him or go to hear him speak. There's no sense of patronizing with Clay, no talking down, nothing beyond the simple facts of his life and how he makes those facts lead to success.

Isn't that the way everything should be?

Also, I want to mention that my wife Irene played a critical role in the writing of this book. She edited, suggested and critiqued well beyond the call of duty. For that I am grateful. If you notice any errors on these pages they only indicate that I failed (after making the mistake in the first place) to correct them after editing. So, I get to own them not once but twice.

Scot Laney
Portland, OR.
January 2, 2008

Forward

If, on a hypothetical lazy summer afternoon, you ease your boat to the back of your favorite cove and Clay Dyer happens to be in it with his boat too, then you might be in for a surprise. You might feel like you may as well be seeing a four hundred pound hamster driving a school bus or a silverback gorilla working the drive-up at the local Steer Burger.

Your eyes are telling your brain what you're looking at, but your brain is slow on the uptake.

In defense of the brain, it makes sense that you should not be seeing there in front of you a man with no legs, no left arm- and only a small appendage where his right arm should be- on the front casting deck of a slicked up Ranger bass boat, working a jig over some brush or a spinner bait on top of a grass bed. Casting by tucking the butt of the rod under his chin and swinging his body in a quick right to left motion. Reeling with the end of his small stump of a right arm. Doing this again and again and always better than you can, unless you happen to be another of the top rated professional anglers in the world.

Because, he is one of those top ranked anglers in the sport of competitive bass fishing. And a sport it is, with two major trails and numerous regional and smaller national trails. Some $50 billion is spent annually chasing the bass fish around, and Clay Dyer-without the use of any prosthetic devices or mechanical aids of any kind-is right in the middle of it all. But fishing is simply what Clay does and, while it explains a little bit about who he is, it does not explain nearly everything.

His story is almost beyond description, almost defies any logic, but is always an inspiration and a primer for all of us on the topics of overcoming adversity, being positive, and never allowing your doubt (or the doubt of anyone else for that matter) to cloud an answer to your own questions.

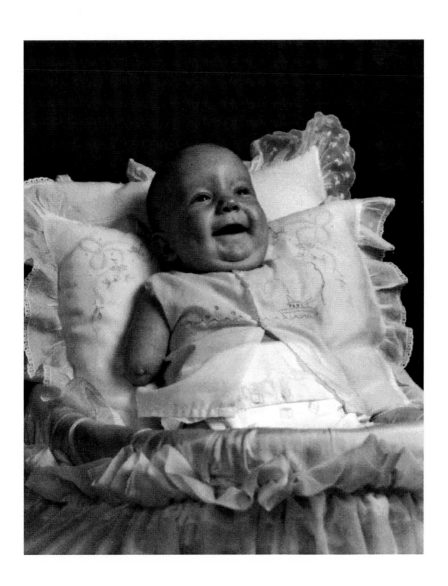

Clay Dyer entered the world on May 23, 1978
with his dad asking one simple question:

"What will life be like for him?"

Clay on Clay:

"I never wanted to be treated different from other kids, I just wanted to do what everyone else did. Plus, I wanted people to look at me doing something and think to themselves that they wanted to do what I did, that they could do things too if they put their mind to it."

The Beginning Time

Hamilton, Alabama shoulders hard to the
Buttahatchee, a river named after a local native tribe that
inhabited the area. The town became famous years ago as a
guaranteed, one day, no hassle supplier of "quickie" divorces
(a fact that landed several Hamilton area barristers in hot
water) and has the distinction of being the largest city in
the U.S. never served by a railroad. Hamilton is on the old
Military Road, the New Orleans-Nashville shortcut built
by Tennessee soldiers returning from the 1815 Battle of
New Orleans. Perhaps-with amazing foresight-the soldiers
knew that, sans ever a railroad, Hamiltonians would have
to walk or ride wherever they went. Or maybe, the tired yet
victorious troops just wanted to get back to hearth and home
a little sooner.

Hamilton is the Marion County seat. Marion County, once one of the largest in the United States, is named for the Revolutionary War hero, Frances Marion, aptly nicknamed "The Swamp Fox" by the British. Presumably, the Redcoats were growing tired of chasing Marion and his troops around the malarial pig mires and dog bogs then dotting the landscape of South Carolina, Marion's home turf. Aptly so, in light of her early association with conflict, the town has a long history of sending her sons and daughters off to war and getting back fewer than went - not so unlike many small towns across the U.S.

Life in Hamilton subscribes to a value set lost in some of the bigger, more urbanized places in the country, a fact that would become very important to the Clarence Dyer family in the years to come for reasons outlined later in this book. Friday nights are reserved for whatever sports the local high school is playing during the school year. Football is a big thing, the law still being the law in Northwest Alabama, and the expectation for the "smash mouth" version of the game is carved in stone. There is an ongoing, but mostly good-natured, debate that involves the various strengths and weaknesses of the University of Alabama as compared to Auburn University. There is little middle ground to be found when the discussion turns to this subject and each side of the argument has assurances from powers divine that their position is the correct one.

Sundays are for church and the chicken roasting in the oven or frying in the pan afterward. The workweek is just that, with the proper emphasis placed on the operative "work" part of the word. People earn their money with elbow grease and honest effort, in the manner that they were raised. Included in the local work mix is a ninth generation potter that still uses a mule named Blue to power his clay mill, but has a company webpage complete with some toe-tapping roots music. Old and new blended together in ways that compliment one another in the information slash hand thrown pottery era.

Not such a bad deal all in all, and not a bad place to hang your hat each evening.

Although no precise records exist, it is a safe bet that prior to May 23, 1978, everyone in Hamilton had been born with a mostly complete set of arms and legs. But certainly not all have managed to keep them through the trials and tribulations of accident and injury, a Civil War, a "War to end all Wars" that did nothing of the sort, another World War, Korea, Vietnam et al.

At least they had them to begin with and that's an important point.

Clayton Andrew Dyer reset the table on that date back in May of 1978, when he became the current leader in the sans arms and legs category.

That is exactly where this story begins.

*****

Pride and Jane Gann
Clay's Maternal Grandparents

Beverly Gann had grown up in Hamilton, the daughter of a world champion raccoon hunter named Pride Gann and his wife Jane. Tenacity is a family trait, and she was raised in an "if you work hard enough, you can do it" environment. Tenacity can also be described as a certain amount of piss and vinegar, and she had her fair share of that too. In 1971, she spotted a new face in town exiting the bank where her mother worked, a "real cute" guy that she did not know. In a small town, a person can be conspicuous merely by his or her presence, and this was the case here. Only after a friend introduced her to the stranger did she find out, in short order, that his name was Clarence Dyer. He had moved to town from Centerville, TN., and he worked in the modular housing business as a salesman. A laid-back sort of fellow, he was in contrast to the Gann clan but certainly not in a bad way.

Apparently the "real cute" observation was mutual, as five months later Beverly became Mrs. Clarence Dyer. A home was set up, and she and Clarence soon started a family with the arrival of a son, Christopher.

Clarence worked, Beverly mothered and returned to school to work on an advanced degree, and Chris got older- as kids do- when the news came, in the fall of 1977, that sometime in the spring Chris would have a brother or sister. "We didn't have all of the tests then that they do now," Beverly says, "so we didn't know if it was a boy or girl or any of the rest of the information you get today." It was the "rest of the information" part of the pregnancy that held the biggest surprise, and the biggest challenge, for the Dyer family. But no one could have known that at the time.

The obstetrician practiced in Amory, Mississippi, and it was there that Clarence and Beverly went when labor came. There had been, lack of available testing or not, no medical signs during the pregnancy that anything was abnormal. There was no reason to suspect that this delivery would be any different than it was with Chris seven years prior.

Except that Beverly had one nagging thought that stayed in the back of her mind, one that she had not readily shared.

Earlier that year she had had a dream, and in the dream her second baby had been born without all of his arms and legs. Looking back on it now, she wonders if this was a message (if maybe an example how these things work in some way) from above to prepare her, or at least to help her cope. There was nothing in the family history to suggest that this would be the case so where had this odd night-fright come from?

Early in the delivery the doctor had a suspicion that the baby was in a breech position. He ordered an x-ray to confirm the position of the fetus as Beverly went further into labor. Clarence was told that the x-ray clearly showed that nothing was right, that something during gestation had gone horribly, terribly, and completely wrong.

He now knew, the doctors and nurses knew, everyone

but Beverly knew. All agreed that this was no time to tell her either. Perhaps, because it fit well with his lower key approach to life in general, this seemed the best way to go to Clarence. In any event, there was no reason for Beverly to know about this then, right in the middle of labor. What would be the point? How would it change anything?

The baby that was coming would be like none other anyone on the delivery team had ever seen before, and there was little chance that any of them had the slightest idea what to do now or after delivery. The x-ray showed, with a clarity that was most cruel under the circumstances, that the baby had no legs, no arms, and was really just a head and a torso with nothing much else save for a small appendage off the right shoulder.

It was what it was, and there would be time for tears later as well as whatever else comes along for the pony ride in a situation such as this. Until then it was a time for prayer and a concern for his wife. Although Clarence knew that he was helpless to really do much at all, he also understood that he would be the one left to figure out how to tell Beverly what had happened when the time came. When she was ready. When she had recovered from the delivery.

When she was strong enough to see her new son.

Naturally, that time did come. Beverly, seen on camera during the filming of an ESPN special segment on Clay recorded in 2006, pulled no punches. When asked about what it felt like to see Clay for the first time she

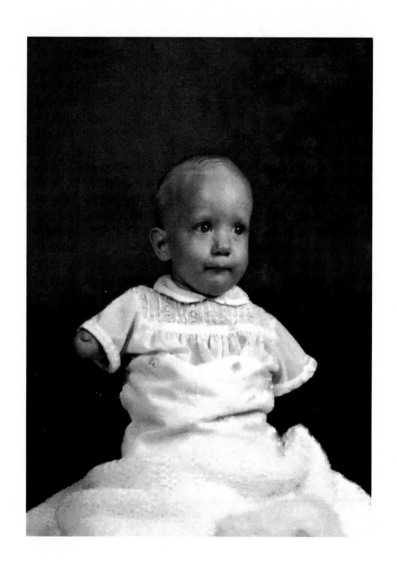

replied through tears, "I almost passed out." Clarence, when asked the same question on the same segment, replied that he was "disappointed" when he first saw his new son. In the way that television can remind us (now and again but not often) just how powerful it can be, the skilled interviewer asked the follow-up question that saved the answer from seeming harsh and cold to the viewer.

"In what way?"

"Because of the things that I thought he would miss out on," Clarence replied.

The doctor returned later to talk with the family about their new baby. He went through the usual list of emotions and what they could expect. Anger, guilt, agony- he ticked them off with a textbook appreciation of the why and how these things work, maybe even some sense of personal experience.

For Clarence and Beverly some things were clear. First, the new family mantra would be something along the lines of, "we'll worry about that later." What about the infant years, what about a toddler who won't be able to toddle, what about school and kids and sports? The "what about" outnumbered the "we know about" 10,000 to 1 and had sent for reinforcements to press the advantage even further.

We'll worry about it later. When it's upon us. But not right now. This was the only defense, the only way to cope with the immediate.

Now we need to concentrate on today, what to do this instant. Foremost, even when the simplest electronic item-a cheap alarm clock or some other doodad- comes with an instruction manual, kids do not. Any kids, let alone kids like Clay, who would need a rather extensive one to say the least if such a thing existed.

It's a measure of how extraordinary these parents are when you see, years later, the results of their effort. Although they would never see it that way, it is a simple enough observation to make. What Clarence and Beverly Dyer did know is that they and the extended family would be on their own making the whole thing up as they went along.

Four days after he was born, with no real sense of what to do except focus on the here and now, the Dyers brought their new son home from the hospital.

*****

Fast forward a few years and you begin to see how the duel influence of family and Hamilton came to play a part, how both contributed to what would be the Dyer's early experience with Clay. In the immediate, after returning home from the hospital, the family staked an inclusive claim on baby Clay. Christopher was excited to have a brother, and Beverly does not remember him asking any questions at all about the baby. For him, he was just Clay, and he would do those things that you do for and with a kid brother. Clarence

Pop Pa & Mom Ma Litton
Clay's Paternal Grandmother and her husband

had lost his own father years ago, but his mother came to stay with him while Beverly was still in the hospital and later when the family came home. Within the family, Clay never became the "elephant in the room." Everyone knew what the score was, and everyone pitched in no differently then they would with any new addition to the family, making bottles, holding the baby, changing diapers, helping in all the ways a person does.

Yet Beverly admits to having some guilt about the birth and wondering if there was something that she did to cause the baby to be born this way. Naturally you would expect any mother to have these feelings, and they would last for years afterward as she worked the details over in her head. It was not an obsession per se but still they were there in the back-and sometimes the front-of her mind.

For his part, Clay acted like any other baby. He would not sleep, instead seeming to spend his time looking around, tracking people as they moved about around him. This was good news, because there was concern about his mental health in light of his physical situation. One had to wonder, with such obvious limitations to his development, what else could be wrong. The nurse at the hospital had told the Dyers that there was nothing to worry about, that mentally Clay was just like any of the thousands of other babies she had seen in the nursery over the years.

Comforting words to be sure. Yet there was also a sense of needing to see for themselves, to get some closure to some lingering questions the family had. But overall it appeared that the initial worry was for naught as Clay developed steadily, a bright eyed and aware baby.

It was during this time that Clarence and Beverly were invited to take Clay to see a medical team that was focused on genetics and the role that genes play in the family tree. Sensing that they wanted to know if there was some sort of genetic mutation and fearful that it had been passed on to Chris and Clay, they agreed. When the two doctors examined Clay they quickly agreed that however it was that Clay developed the way that he did, it was not genetically related. They had no answer for the "why," but the news went a long way in answering the "why not." Finally, both parents could feel comfortable that there was no boogieman buried in the family DNA, nothing that would appear again and again in the future, a welcome "we know about".

*****

It was also during this time that Clay began to show some signs of his capacity to improvise solutions to problems that presented themselves. Clarence and Beverly began taking Clay to a clinic in Michigan every three months. The clinic would evaluate Clay for different prosthetic devices that were being developed. At one point, Clay was fitted with a mechanical left arm. The arm required Clay to use his small right arm appendage to manipulate the new device. Although he did master the device, it was soon agreed by all that, while it gave Clay some additional

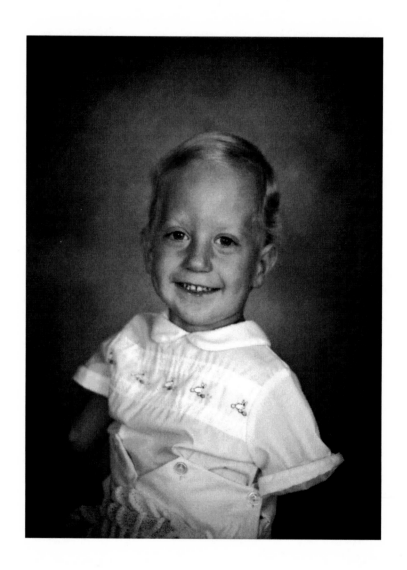

capacity, the net result was that he was able to do fewer things with it than without so the arm was discarded. Also joining the scrap heap after a time was his sway walker, a device that allowed him to walk by swinging his torso around in a way that moved some large "feet" on the bottom of the contraption. Clay could make better time on his own by scooting along the floor balanced on the bottom of his torso.

On one occasion, a local Michigan newspaper came to the clinic to write a feature article about Clay getting his first motorized wheelchair. Controlled by a joystick arrangement, the wheelchair was complex and normally required a great deal of training to use with any degree of safety. While the reporter for the paper gathered around and the photographer checked his camera settings, the person charged with the training explained the various difficulties of mastering the equipment in front of them. For his part, Clay jumped onboard, flipped the power switch on, and drove off down the hall. Executing a perfect u-turn, Clay returned, backed the chair up to the wall, and flipped the power off, ready to receive his training in the proper use of the device.

Clay was five years old.

On another occasion, Clay was pestering Clarence to teach him how to use a bait-casting reel. Clarence and Clay spent time fishing in a little pond in the evenings after Clarence had returned home from work. Naturally Clay was outfitted early on with a Zebco 303, that most familiar reel of choice for beginning anglers. He taught himself to

use it, which is amazing enough under the circumstances. How many people have learned to fish with a Zebco closed face spinning reel is a great mystery, not unlike how many angels can dance on the head of a pin, or why the ABC's are in the order they are, most people in general agreement that it's because of that song. But a bait-casting reel is another subject altogether. Bait casters are the big leagues of fishing reels. They are difficult to use, and many adults never master the art of the bait-cast; the spool control, the thumb pressure applied at just the right instant, how to make a bird's nest look natural, like you intended to do it, just a little "professional overrun."

But each night Clay would insist that Clarence teach him how to use one. Clarence was naturally hesitant to do so. The learning curve can be long and frustrating under the best of circumstances. But Clay was convinced that he could make it work. Already Clay had developed a keen sense for argument, always ready with primary, secondary and extemporaneous versions all designed to help you, the listener, see his point.

One night, as they prepared to go to the pond, Clay chose a rod equipped with a bait-casting reel to use. Clarence didn't say anything and thought that he would go ahead and let Clay get this out of his system. Arriving at the pond Clarence watched from the corner of his eye as Clay positioned himself for a cast, which turned out to be perfectly placed.

Without another word Clay said simply: "I figured

that out while you were at work."

So even with the mountain of questions that still surrounded the Dyer family everyday, it was becoming apparent that Clay was not simply going to take things at face value. While both Beverly and Clarence had natural trepidations about certain things, Clay did not necessarily always share these.

Even though he was still just a little boy, Clay was already in the habit of working on the skills he would need by himself and on his own. School was on the horizon. Clay would need to refine these skills even more in the years ahead.

Clay on School:

"When I went to school I wasn't certain about what to expect. I didn't know about what it would be like, how my classmates would see me. But I wanted to go. I knew that I could do it. When I met my teacher, and my aid, things looked like they would be okay."

Just Like Any Kid

As Clay got older, it was time to start doing the things that kids do including go to school, play sports as well as begin the long process of becoming who you are and what you will become. In short, it was time to start making some decisions, and these decisions would carry implications for the present as well as the future.

Clay had never been shielded from the public in any way. He went with his parents and brother everywhere they went, carried from place to place; the church, the store and ball games. The people of Hamilton never seemed to make much of a deal one way or the other about Clay once the initial reactions wore away. As far as the town was concerned, he was just another kid, and he was treated that way. In large part because of this Clay never saw himself as different either. Granted, he could look in a mirror and see things for himself. Occasionally another kid would say something to him, something like, "You don't have any arms and legs." Clay would just shake his head in amazement. "Really?" he would reply, "I never knew that." Sometimes he would look down and feign surprise. "What happened to my arms and legs, they were here just a minute ago." But rather than taunts, these comments tended to be examples of the simple nature that kids have with one another where even the obvious needs to be commented on or explained in some way so that it becomes familiar. Kids just acting like kids. Adults can take this for more than it is, but kids just have a natural curiosity about things, and Clay must have looked to them how they sometimes felt themselves: less than complete and dealing with a world that was big, sometimes scary, and tough to negotiate. Clarence knew that sometimes when they would take Clay to Birmingham or other places kids would be apprehensive, at times pointing at him or making comments to one another. Clarence would resist the urge to tell them to stop or to say something to their parents. But those were the outsiders, the kids from other places. They weren't comfortable with Clay. He wasn't a part of the day-to-day landscape like he was at home in Hamilton, and Clarence knew this. He also knew that if they really did know his son, the questions and stares would go away eventually. Clay would win them over or put their minds at ease.

Beverly will tell you that every time an obstacle confronted them, a solution would present itself soon enough, and the family had great faith in this seemingly cosmic system of problems followed by solutions or resolutions. For a family of deep faith, it was clear that God had a plan and was calling the shots.

School, and what to do about it, was one of these subjects that had become common over the years. It went without saying that Clay would need some help navigating the classroom. How would he get to his desk, go out for recess, participate in classroom activities? But it was never an issue that he would not go to school along with the rest of the kids. In most places today, Clay would have been showered with various labels and acronyms all designed by the well-meaning to be helpful. In reality, this set of labels sometimes can become anything but. They can define a child as something quantitative and not qualitative and provide for a lifetime of meeting expectations that have been set artificially low and out of the mainstream of society. But mainstreaming was not an issue in Hamilton, where there was just one stream, and you better be ready to swim in it.

A teacher named Betty Fowler provided the floatation that Clay would need; and a local woman, Nancy Logan, made sure there was river rescue available, just in case.

People who know Betty Fowler describe her as a "dream teacher," an "extremely kind person" who is possessed of a gentle and caring soul. High tribute in small town America and only given to those who earn it. It seems like everyone has a certain teacher that they look back upon years later and appreciate the things they did for them, the

Betty Fowler

influence that they had over them. Good teachers-and we're lucky that in our society we have many to choose from-seem to be able to see a certain bright light in children, know how to make that light shine, know how to draw out the best from inside each child. It becomes a common theme when talking with people that Betty has this gift.

Clay was certainly not unknown to Betty. As a teenager Beverly had babysat for Betty and her husband Edward, a local attorney, when the Fowler kids were younger. When Clay was born Betty knew the circumstances, staying in touch in the years leading up to Clay starting school.

Betty knew what her role would be when that time came too.

Betty had started teaching years before Clay came along. Although she originally had a business background, it was through her work with the young kids in church that she began to sense that she had a calling beyond the horizons of a Profit and Loss statement, one not so easily fitted to a balance sheet or weekly sales report. She got the necessary additional college courses that focused on early education and went to work in the public school. When the time came, she insisted to the school administration that she get Clay in her class, because no teacher yet had been "blessed with a student like Clay." Plus, she had a plan for him. Like Beverly and Clarence, she knew that no cookbook existed to show her how to bake this cake. She knew that there were no roadmaps to navigate with, nothing beyond a good teacher's sense of what would work. But that was enough, with one additional stipulation: Betty would be allowed to hand pick an aide for Clay, and the woman she had in mind was not even in the business. Nancy Logan was her name, and the initial problem was that no one knew with any certainty that she would do it. What they had in mind for Mrs. Logan was a lot to ask of anyone.

But this was Hamilton, and there always is a way to get things done in a town where even Blue the mule works every day.

Nancy Logan had taught Sunday school with Betty Fowler for years prior to Clay's birth. By all accounts they were a good team, a fixture at the Baptist church attended by the two women and the Dyer family. Although she had not been around him much, Nancy knew about Clay and remembered that when he was born the town was in shock. Most people wondered what would happen in the future.

Nancy had dropped out of college to marry her husband Steve. Steve owned a mobile home manufacturing company in town, later becoming a State Representative and then the mayor of Hamilton. When Clay was ready to enter kindergarten, Nancy and Steve had three children of their own, and Nancy was a full time mother to them. So when the principal at Hamilton Elementary called one day and explained the situation to her, that Betty had requested her specifically to be Clay's full time classroom aid, Nancy was unprepared to answer. Initially she thought that she was not adequately trained for such a huge responsibility. Beyond

Nancy Logan

the fact that the youngest Logan child was not school age yet, the middle child would just be starting the next year. It wasn't the perfect time to give oneself over to a project like the one proposed to her. Yet she had an inkling that this was the right thing to do. Again, those small town values shining through in the way they would over and over for Clay.

She told Principal Clark that she would discuss it with her husband and get back to him. She also made a new entry at the top of her personal prayer list and would ask God what she should do.

For his part, Steve told her that this might be a project that she would want to get involved with, one that would make a lasting difference to Clay. For His part, God replied to her prayers telling her to get with the program, that she could do this.

The deal was set; the gentile teacher with a plan and the lady with a huge heart and no formal training would become central figures in the Dyer family for the next nine years and beyond. The Fowler-Logan machine was oiled, cranked, and on the field.

*****

Beverly brought Clay in to the classroom on the first day of school and set him on the floor. Prior to this point Nancy had never really had a good look at the child she was taking charge of. Looking down she remembers what she describes as this "little lump of a boy" there on the floor.

"Can you imagine," she asked when interviewed, "no arms and no legs? He was so tiny, just a little boy." Beverly did what all parents do on the first day of school and left young Clay there, although it must have been agonizing to do so. His future now spread out before him in the hands of these two amazing women. No one knew what to expect. No one was certain what would happen.

Nancy looked down and saw tears, "as big as silver dollars," running down Clay's tiny cheeks. No sobbing, but just these huge tears silently dripping to the floor. Clay was frightened by his new surroundings, and Nancy gulped down a good dose of the same feeling herself. Bending over to speak with Clay, she uttered the first words Clay heard from his new aid:

"Clay, Miss Logan is here to help. I promise I will be as nice to you as I am to my own children."

Clay straightened up, wiped the tears from his face with his stump, and started school.

Betty and Nancy agreed early on that Clay would not be treated any differently than the other kids. They had the same expectations of Clay that they had for any of the children. Clay would participate in every activity, every lesson. Nancy knew her role as his aid. She would leave the teaching to Betty and concentrate on physically helping

Clay maneuver around the classroom. She would take him to lunch and physical education, out to recess and to the bathroom. She would not help him with his studies unless the other kids had the same access to individual tutoring. She might help him find his pencil, but Clay had to do the writing. She may put the math lesson in front of him, but Clay had to add the numbers together and fill in the answer.

Clay quickly grew accustomed to the school environment. He could print as well as most of the kids by tucking a pencil under his chin and leaning close to the paper. Betty Fowler insists that he had the neatest handwriting she had ever seen before or since. People today are still somewhat taken aback when Clay signs an autograph for them using his special chin writing technique.

Gradually Betty and Nancy noticed an unexpected development as the year went by. Clay was becoming a leader in the classroom. The other kids went to him with problems they had, and Clay was always receptive to helping them. Clay worried when something went wrong for one of them. Both women agreed that Clay seemed to be shaped by both nature and nurture to be a success, that when he was created he may have missed the arms and legs line because he was busy going through the guts and backbone line several times.

Today, Betty says that Clay taught them all that sometimes we get so caught up in our physical appearance that we forget what our true calling is.

The two women also made another mutual observation. Clay was a good student and worked hard in school even though, Nancy admits, he may not have always liked it. But something burned inside the little boy, even at this young age. Although he was resigned to the fact that he had to go to school, Clay often stared out the window.

Clay wanted to be outside, out in the fresh air. Given a choice, Clay would go outside and never come inside. When the other kids laid down for a nap after lunch, Clay would fiddle with his little rest mat flopping from side to side begging Nancy to take him out. Everything he liked to do was outside. He was already learning to fish a little bit, and Clarence and Pride Gann were making sure Clay knew that there were plenty of topics to be discussed in the field as well as the classroom.

Looking back, it seems as if Clay had already made some decisions about where he would go in life, and it wasn't going to be under a roof or surrounded by walls.

*****

There is a story told about the Studebaker Wagon Company. The company became famous later as one of the early and more successful manufacturers of automobiles. At a time when corporations were establishing themselves with extensive and complex articles of incorporation, the Studebaker brothers were rather short and to the point in their filing, paraphrased here as this:

"I, Jacob Studebaker, promise to sell all the wagons my brothers Clement and John can make. We, Clement and John Studebaker, promise to make all the wagons Jacob can sell."

Why clutter the landscape when simplicity will serve just as well? In this sort of Studebaker-ish way, Nancy and Clay also came to an agreement early on in that first year of kindergarten. Clay promised that he would try anything. Nancy promised that she would help in any way that she could. By this simple promise, wagons were made and sold that year at Hamilton Elementary.

At the midpoint of the school year, Betty received a notification that nominations were due for a national award called, "Yes, I Can!" The Yes I Can Foundation, a part of the Council for Exceptional Children that honors children with disabilities who have made significant achievements administers the yearly award. Each year up to twenty-seven international winners are selected for accomplishments in academics, the arts, athletics, community service and other categories. Betty wondered if Clay would qualify for the award and discussed it with Nancy. Betty decided that she would nominate Clay and see what would happen. Based on the details that she provided to the judges' panel, Clay was selected as one of the winners for that year.

Clay does not remember much about the awards ceremony which was held in Washington D.C. Beverly Dyer notes that Linda Carter, the star of the Wonder Woman series on television, presented the award to Clay and this made a lasting impression, she assumes, on Clarence. For his part, Clarence doesn't comment one way or the other, having not just recently fallen off the back of a turnip truck.

In any event, it was national recognition of Clay and an honor for the entire family. More importantly, on the local level, at the end of the school year Clay was chosen by the other children to play the coveted role of the farmer in the annual classroom play. The farmer got to dress up in a straw hat and cover-alls, chew on a piece of straw in the way farmers are imagined to, had a speaking part, and was all the rage in thespian kindergarten circles that year. It was a huge honor, and Clay played the part with relish, bellowing out his lines for all to hear.

Betty and Nancy were cultivating the first tiny glimpse of the performer within the little boy and the light within him.

*****

Each year for the next eight years, Nancy and Clay would continue with this arrangement- Nancy providing the heavy lifting and toting, Clay the studying and determination to do his best. Nancy would meet with Clay's new teacher before the school year and together they would make a plan that allowed Nancy to do her job with the least distraction to

the teacher and other students. Every year the duo was faced
with a few new students, and Nancy would make certain that
the kids understood that Clay, although physically different
from them, also had his own skills and talents just like they
did. For the most part, the other kids, as always, seemed to
accept Clay at face value. Nancy does not ever remember
other kids that were mean to him, at least not in a way that
was different than kids can sometimes be mean to others.
He was never picked on or made fun of that she is aware of.
Never was he pushed to the side. Clay always seemed to be
right in the middle of things, and his recess play sessions
became the social place to be, where all were welcome.
Clay would line the kids up on an embankment on the side
of the school, and they would roll down it or play with the
supply of model cars that Clay had brought from home.
Clay was always reminding Nancy not to forget his football
helmet, that there was a game to play, and he was going
to be the quarterback which he often was. According to
Nancy, one might imagine that Clay would run a somewhat
limited offense. Power a few running plays up the middle or
around the end. But, the fact is, he taught himself to throw a
pretty decent spiral pass and was not afraid to go deep if he
had a good receiver with decent speed. Clay would tell his
teachers and the other kids that someday he might play in
the NFL, not an uncommon claim from little boys his age.
But with Clay, the trouble you had hearing that as an adult
was, while you knew certainly this would never be the case,
you also had to think that if any no-legged player without
arms ever did make the big show, it would probably be him.

Outside of school, Clay and a gang of kids from the

neighborhood would get together after class or on weekends. They would hang around one or the other's houses, mess around in the woods, or go fishing. Nathan Brown and Carl Berryhill became close friends with Clay; the core of what later would become a partner's team in local bass tournaments in the area. More importantly, later on they would share in some events in high school that were a watershed for Clay and served to refocus his energy in a direction that even he must have thought was, at the very best, a long shot.

*****

Nancy left the Dyer-Logan team at the end of the eighth grade. The decision to do so was difficult at the time. Today, she admits that she wishes she had remained with Clay through high school. However, at the time she was concerned that Clay needed a male aid in school. She worried that he might become embarrassed having a woman following him around, especially when it came to dating, a subject that Clay showed an early-and still current-aptitude for. As Clay cites Nancy and Betty as two of the people that have helped make him who he is today, the outsider is left believing that he probably did not have the same issues that Nancy did at the time. But Nancy made the decision then that she would leave Clay, let him spread his wings with a new aid, and pray for the best. Besides, another child that was just starting school that year, a young girl with spinal bifida, needed Nancy. Nancy would go and help her the same way that she helped Clay, and Clay would move on without her. Nancy ended up working with the girl in the same capacity through fifth grade.

Clay had a group of buddies to hang around with and bounce things off. He was having, what anyone would say, was a typical experience in school. In some ways, it seemed to Nancy that Clay no longer needed her. If there is any truth in that, it is only because Nancy had done such an incredible job preparing Clay for high school. In any event, the decision was made, and Clay was assigned a new aid, a woman. So in the end, he did not end up with a male aid anyway, and although this new woman was perfectly competent, Nancy felt as if Clay needed something different, that the new situation still left him vulnerable to embarrassment when it was time to use the bathroom or ask a girl to the prom. But the deck chairs were lined up, and off to high school Clay went.

Clay on High School:

*"I know this may surprise a lot of people,
but my biggest concern entering high school was
the academic challenge. I made good grades in
elementary school, but I knew the courses would be
much tougher in high school. I hadn't let a challenge
beat me before, and I was determined that I would rise
to the challenge academically."*

U-Turn

For most people, the high school experience falls roughly within three distinct camps: the people that look back on it with a longing for those days, the people that look back on it with a definite absence of that longing, and the majority of people that could not really care less one way or the other.

Although everyone has his or her own personal memories and feelings associated with what has been described as the mouse race that trains you for the lifelong rat race later, most would agree that perhaps a true definition of terror would be to wake up one morning and discover that your high school class is running the country. In any event, high school has all of the necessary elements to go terribly wrong for some, unexpectedly well for others, and proceed forward in a steady yet plodding rate for most, the students clumped together in sort of arbitrary groups built on common interests or self preservation.

Clay entered Hamilton High School happily anticipating the experience, but somewhat unsettled about the more difficult classroom academic requirements, especially since he would not have Nancy pushing him to excel as in the past. There was no concern by him about where he would fit in, having already clustered together his group of guys that loved hunting and fishing, at a high school that appreciated those activities at face value. Again, Hamilton played a role. At most high schools in urban areas, you can look long and hard to find anyone that fishes, and hunting (or even the mention of same) is discouraged by school administrations that feel somehow enlightened but, in fact, are ignorant of the subject altogether. In his General Introduction to Psychoanalysis, Sigmund Freud writes on the subject of hunting that "a fear of weapons is a sign of retarded emotional and sexual maturity." It is reasonably argued that the people so suffering seem to be attracted to school administration and running for the local school board in America's bigger cities and suburbs. But certainly in Hamilton, Alabama, the social enlightenment train had not shown up, perhaps because of the previously mentioned lack of service. In Hamilton, there are numerous examples of students that were benefited by this general lack of political correctness.

Clay and his group went to football games,

participated in class, and chased girls around like most high school boys do. On weekends, they went fishing, participating in local bass tournaments as a team. Fishing and hunting are competitive activities in many places, perhaps throwbacks to the time in human evolution when the man that could hunt or fish the best usually got the girl, or several of them- depending on which primitive man theory you throw in with- thus allowing his genes to be carried forward through the ages. It also helped if you could make fire and were handy with a flint axe. Being kind, caring, and a good listener came much later, well after the food, shelter, and general herd health issues became less desperate, and the human race had learned to communicate in something other than a series of throaty grunts.

It was during this time that Clay was becoming increasingly more serious about his fishing. The best gear and all of the new techniques being reported in the magazines caught his attention. His eye for high-end rods and reels was outstripping his ability to pay for them; and often he would go hat-in-hand to his parents with yet another request for some new equipment.

On one occasion, he noticed a rod and reel combination in a catalog. It was the most beautiful thing he had ever laid eyes on, well-balanced and meticulously made, and he wore the ink off the page looking at it. Soon he realized that he just had to have it. He constructed a short, yet persuasive, argument about why he needed this particular rod and reel even though he had several others already. One evening he sensed the timing was right and approached

Clarence about it as they watched television. He made his case, but his dad was having nothing of it, pointing to all of the equipment Clay already owned. Clarence asked the question that bass anglers worldwide dread hearing, usually from a wife:

"Exactly how much stuff does one guy need to bass fish anyway?"

Clay could see that his primary line of reasoning was falling apart like a cheap suit. His secondary argument, based loosely on the theory that the people he was competing against were also so equipped with the best equipment thus it was an issue of being at least as well armed, seemed to be a non-starter. Appealing to his mother on the other end of the couch didn't crack any new holes in the ice either. All that was left was to bring out the big guns. "Mom," he said, "just think of all the money I've saved you on shoes!"

UPS delivered the new rod and reel later that week, and Clay still has it today.

Still all was not perfect in Clay's world. Granted, he was living a typical high school experience and that alone was cause for celebration. He was also typical in other less than perfect ways, too. Like many kids will, Clay soon found himself doing some things he was not really proud of. Some things that he knew were wrong, but also seemed not so out of the ordinary. Clay began to exert his independence by staying out late, drinking and partying with his friends. He was making some bad choices, and he knew it. Clay won't cop to peer pressure like some will. He knew that he had freedom of choice. The decisions were his, and he knew they were wrong. Nonetheless, he found himself running with a fast crowd, doing what they did, sometimes the ringleader and other times just part of the circus. It was all in good fun, but none of it the right thing to be doing. For the first time in his life, Clay began to worry that maybe he wasn't as in control as he thought. Perhaps life could be a little more to chew at times than he could handle. Accustomed to having the answers, to figuring out the solutions with the people around him or on his own, Clay was in a spot that was new to him. Knowing this, the question became a simple one: How would he get out?

*****

Once again, the answer presented itself soon enough. It was to be a totally new direction for Clay, a merge from the road he was on to a new road he had not fully traveled before. Most interesting was the fact that, unlike prior instances, the formation of the general plan as presented had nothing to do with direct input from Clay. This would not be a problem that Clay determined the correct course of action to solve. After being present all of his life, after providing so many things to Clay along the way like a strong family, a decent place to grow up and certainly Betty Fowler and Nancy Logan, the man upstairs was calling, and He was calling collect.

The concept of God-really religion in general-in this country is complex. It's a topic that is both deeply personal yet debated publicly all the time. At the very dawn of the United States, religion became one of the topics that almost toppled the new nation before the opening bell could even be rung. The debate about religion in society went on for several weeks. The founding fathers were roiled in argument over what part it would play. In an ironic twist, a compromise was made. No religion would be anointed the "official" religion of the republic, in the fashion of the Church of England, the very source of bitter divide that sent the Pilgrims, after several interim stops and much persecution along the way, to our shores in the first place. A separation of church and state was agreed upon. If only these men could see us now and discover the limits the clause has been expanded to. One can imagine that George Washington, never one to swear, would probably pop off a few good ones. Never was it the intent to banish God from the proper and civil governing of the nation. But that's a topic for another time. For now, let it suffice to say that all peoples are free to come to whatever form of relationship they want with God, or none at all, if they are particularly adventuresome.

The simple fact remains that when God thumped Clay over the head, it made a lasting impression, like it does anyone that bothers to listen when it happens. Clay's story cannot be told without including the simple fact that he was issued a wake-up call that eventually put him on a path to success. Once Lee Trevino, after having been struck by lightning on the golf course, remarked that when God wants to play through you better let Him. Good advice. In this case, the message that came down was really more one that God wanted Clay to play through, and he better get moving.

Clay had grown up in a church-going family and had attended church for as long as he can recall. However, attending church and living the word can be two different things. While Clay was good about being in church, he admits that he was not really of church. He was not living life to the fullest extent that God wanted him to and wished for him to do. Soon after graduation from high school that changed.

About a month after graduation, Clay was invited by a friend to attend a youth rally at a local church. On the morning of the rally, Clay awoke with an unusual feeling of anxiety about the event that began later that evening. He found that he was nervous, even fearful, about going. There was no particular reason for this, yet his feelings were real. As the day wore on, these feelings became more acute. Clay began to fear that he was having a heart attack or other serious problem with his health. Yet, he made the decision that he would attend the rally regardless.

During the service, Clay listened to several personal testimonies followed by some dramatic performances, and then a short devotional. His previous feelings from earlier in the day became almost overwhelming, and soon Clay started thinking that he had never felt so miserable and out of sorts in his whole life. He was also more than just a little scared about what may be happening to him, still wondering if he was having a medical emergency, if he should ask to be taken to the hospital, or maybe just bolt from the church. There was nothing to pin the feelings on directly. They were just there, and he felt terrible.

At the conclusion of the rally, the minister offered an invitation to come forward to those that wanted to. Many people started to find their way down the aisle to the front of the church, Clay among them. It seemed like the thing to do, if for no other reason than to join the crowd of kids at the front. While waiting there, Clay felt a hand on his shoulder that made him jump. His friend had approached him from behind, and Clay had not seen him coming. To the friend, it was obvious that something was wrong with Clay. Something was bothering him although Clay tried to convince him that this was not the case, that he felt fine. The friend then asked Clay that if something were to happen to Clay that night, would Clay be going to heaven? It was certainly an oddball question at the end of what had been an oddball day. Clay thought for a moment and told his friend that yes, he guessed that he would go to heaven if something happened that night. Considering how he felt at that exact moment, this might have been a distinct possibility. The Hoover administration, four seasons of the Seinfeld show, and the entire 1962 New York Mets roster had been built on less irony, so anything was possible. But the friend was persistent, wondering why Clay only guessed that he would go to heaven, why he could not be certain. Clay had no good answer, but something clicked for him when the friend asked the question. Clay realized that he needed a much stronger commitment to God if he was going to get anywhere in life. More importantly, he knew that God had expectations of him. He knew that he was put here for a reason, beyond being the kid that makes hay even with a certain lack of farm equipment. As he and his friend prayed, Clay felt God enter his life, and he was immediately healed of his torments from earlier in the day. Clay felt an instantaneous sense of love and peace come over him. Praying there to accept Christ as his savior. It seemed that this prayer was immediately accepted. In the coming few months, Clay worked on his newfound relationship with God. He studied the Bible and allowed his church experience to expand and become more personal.

More importantly, the kid with the largest dose of get up and go, the kid with the steeled resolve to do all things on his terms, his timeline and his rules, sort of went away. In his place rose a kid that would do it God's way.

Soon Clay had a vision, a dream like his mother had had years earlier and another one of those events that make an author's life easier because the drama simply just presents itself. Like his mother's dream before he was born, the dream was about Clay, but this time the kid with no arms and legs was wearing a uniform covered in sponsor logos. Clay only knew of two professions that this would apply to- NASCAR drivers and professional bass fisherman. Although he had actually driven cars in the past, even on one occasion backing a friend's boat trailer into the garage when the task proved too difficult for his buddy, Clay suspected that Richard Childress or Joe Gibbs could view the lack of a driver's license as a negative.

The truth was that Clay, driver's license or not, had already considered a career in fishing. There is a popular creed among bass fishermen that goes something like this:

"Please don't tell my mother I'm a professional fisherman. She thinks I play piano in a brothel."

That one always brings a nervous jitter of laughter from the troops, a joke that is a little too close to home to get an honest peel from the men (and a few women) that actually are professional anglers. These issues aside, Clay was growing increasingly convinced that this was what he was supposed to be doing, that somehow he could reach people through fishing in service to God. He had already discussed the matter with his two fishing friends, Nathan and Carl. Both of them had been supportive of the idea and thought that Clay had the skills to fish for money against the best in the world. Youthful thinking maybe, but the truth was that Clay was a good angler and had been successful in the local events he had participated in. Except that a local derby is a long way from the world inhabited by the marquee names in the sport. Men that had been at the game for a long time and were as skilled at their chosen sport as any other top rated professional is in his or hers.

Plus, there was the added problem of telling your mother the truth. That you are not, as it turns out, a piano player in a brothel.

Dyer Family

Clay on Professional Fishing:

"*I have a drive for competition and a passion for the outdoors. This profession gives me the opportunity to prove to myself and others that God gave me all I need to follow my passion and compete with the best in the world on a level playing field without any accommodations. The fish don't know, or care, that I don't have limbs.*"

Starting Down the Road

Clarence and Beverly had always worried about what Clay would do for a living and who would take care of him, along with the host of other things to be worked out. As time went on, Clay demonstrated his ability to overcome obstacles on his own. How do you teach a kid like Clay to throw a football, shoot a basketball, and brush his teeth? The short answer is that you don't. All these things are worked out through a sort of jumbo game of trial and error, bruises, and picking yourself up to try again.

Making a living, and the subsequent feeling of self-empowerment that comes along with it, is no game. Strong men and women are ruined all the time by the simple act of trying to keep the kids fed, gas in the car, and the bill collectors a livable distance away from the front door. The twist was that Clay wanted to become a professional bass fisherman, an occupation that is notoriously difficult. Clay had announced this to his parents one night at the dinner table, the place where business of this nature took root in the Dyer house.

Dominated by a few anglers at the very top of the sport (millionaires all but the definite exception to the masses of others slugging it out for the scraps), bass fishing has kicked able men to the curb with disturbing regularity over the last thirty years. In short, not a career choice that normally brings a glint of optimism to the eyes of mothers and fathers. A simple statement of fact for anyone contemplating a career as a professional bass angler would be to first develop a secondary skill, a fallback plan.

Ditch digging comes to mind, and this is not meant to be a slight to ditch diggers the world over.

Comparatively speaking, ditch digging is where the money is between the two. To make the situation more expedient, you may also consider simply giving your tournament entry fees directly to Kevin VanDam, Jay Yelas, Mike Iaconelli, Skeet Reese or any of the dozen or so other top ranked professionals that seem to win the alpha chimp's share of the spoils. As a newcomer, making your way up the ranks, you can be certain that, of the $40 billion or so that changes hands in bass fishing each year, your share will be close to none. However, your cost to win that chunk of nothing will be significant, even mind boggling, if you are very honest with yourself. But it was in to this morass that Clay wanted to throw himself. Beyond even all that, he had decided to do so without the aid of any prosthetic devices.

Both Clarence and Beverly outwardly supported his decision. On the inside, the usual feelings of concern for Clay started their incessant rumblings once again. How could Clay possibly make this work? How would the other anglers accept him? Could he compete? Would the powers that be let him compete? All of these questions and doubts were there, grinding away at the decision that Clay had made. Beyond all of that, Clarence and Beverly knew that they needed to become more informed about how the sport works. They needed to learn the landscape, understand the commitment and the costs involved.

Although they had serious doubts about the legitimacy of Clay's plan, they outwardly supported him, just like they always had in the past. Besides, Clay had proven their doubts wrong so many times before, what about this would be any different? Clarence and Beverly set about becoming experts on the business of professional bass fishing.

*****

Professional bass fishing is a lot like professional baseball. There are minor leagues (regional and national A, Double A, Triple A) that lead to the major leagues of bass fishing, the Wal-Mart FLW Tour and Series and the

ESPN BASS Elite Series. There are professional tours in the U.S., Japan, Mexico, Spain, Italy, South Africa, Australia, Canada, and still other countries-even Zimbabwe. You can be forgiven if you have never heard of, or have never seen, the sport before on television. A sort of super-size niche, professional bass fishing is very popular-some would argue unnaturally popular-to a limited number of people. The people that are aware of it and follow it are some of the most devoted fans of any sport anywhere. They tend to talk about, debate about, and think about bass fishing at levels previously reserved for more serious topics like medical research, federal monetary policy, or even NASCAR. They go on bass fishing chat rooms like the Bassfishinghomepage.com and tear one another, the leagues, and the anglers to pieces, but all in good, clean fun. They read BassFan.com like a morning newspaper and tear it to pieces in the reader feedback area. All in all, they're a very passionate group of people, good folk that you would call first if you ever had trouble, because you know that they would help in spades.

To compete as an angler, you must work your way up from the bottom to the top. You must succeed at each level, leading to a qualification to compete at the next higher level and spend ever more money doing it. But at any level, no matter how lowly the tour you are fishing, if you are entered as a pro (vs. the non-professional co-angler participant that has to keep quiet and stay in the back of the boat) you are a professional angler, even if on a part-time basis. This means you get to fish from the front of the boat, cover yourself with sponsor patches head to toe if you choose to (not predicated by actually having a sponsorship deal with said sponsor) and generally be known around your workplace as a pretty good angler, the guy to ask if anyone has a fishing question. The vast majority of professional anglers in the United States are just that, and bass fishing is not a full-time job for them. Fewer than 400 professional bass anglers in the world are full-time anglers fishing the highest level of the sport.

Professional bass fishermen make money by finishing high enough in a tournament to win a share of the payout, a portion of the money paid in entry fees that gets returned to the anglers. How high you finish is based on the aggregate weight of your fish over the course of the event. Each day your five biggest fish caught (and kept alive by a complex system of water and oxygen in your boat) are weighed and released back to the lake after the weigh-in ceremony at the end of the day.

If this sounds a bit like gambling, the point is conceded to you without argument. At the higher reaches of the sport, a portion of the money paid by companies that sponsor the tournament trail itself augments the entry fee money. Anglers can make additional money from the sponsors that they work with if their performance on the tour makes them attractive enough to land a sponsor to begin with.

Bass fishing is the last great bargain in advertising if a company happens to make a product that bass fishermen want or need. Although it may be easy to stereotype the sport and the anglers, the fact is that professional bass fishermen tend to be better educated and (at the level where they still have a regular job day-to-day) more highly compensated than the average American. You really can't be a professional angler without some extra money that won't fit in the already filled with money hole you previously dug in your backyard. Bass fishing is a hobby and compulsive illness of the mind neatly packaged together. For those that do it, can't help but do it, nothing else in the world compares.

Bass fishing is a tempting, demanding, and wicked mistress (for the men that do it) or gigolo (for the women professionals) with some tough requirements if you want to stay in her or his good graces, foremost among these are the startup costs.

Bass boats have evolved from simple machines with small outboard motors to complex floating platforms of grace, beauty, and knuckle white performance. Capable of speeds approaching 80 mph, tournament boats are built for performance and durability. The modern tour style bass boat is decked out in elaborate sponsor wraps like a NASCAR and promotes products ranging from auto insurance to pet food with any number of stops between. Still largely individually made, these boats carry a host of advanced electronics to help find the fish and sophisticated livewell systems to keep them alive once you catch them.

Powered by advanced outboard engines built by Mercury, Yamaha, or Evinrude and rated up to 250 horsepower, a fully rigged Ranger, Bass Cat, Nitro, Triton or

Skeeter looks like a caged animal sitting on its custom made trailer- anxious to go out and hunt on the wind. Once on the water, they look menacing, like a shark or a barracuda, perfectly designed and developed for one thing only: the pursuit of a little green and black or sometimes brown and black fish.

Occasionally, a pack of teenagers, out for a romp in daddy's ski boat with radio blaring and nautical rules stowed well out of reach, will come across a tour boat underway across the lake. Although generally having the run of the water, the ski boat soon disappears to the rear of the bass boat with a few choice teenager gestures tossed in the mix for good measure.

To get in the game as an entry-level angler, be certain to reserve about $45,000 for this essential piece of equipment.

The tow vehicle is yet another necessary and expensive piece of gear you will need to buy. All the usual suspects are included here, large trucks and SUV's capable of towing fairly large boats for long distances comfortably and safely. About 100 gallons of fuel will fill both up, and the stops to do this will be frequent. So frequent, in fact, that in vying for your business, Exxon will offer to send you on exotic vacations and Chevron will pay for your children's college tuition. Not true, but you will feel as if they should.

Throw another $45,000 on the pile here.

The gear that a professional angler needs is extensive: rods and reels by the dozen, soft plastic baits, hard baits, top water baits, spinner baits, secret baits that you buy in back alleys in the dark of night, anchor systems, buoy systems, nets, boat hooks, bumpers, life vests, cushions. The list is more extensive than this, but the assumption here is that you get the drift. All this gear is neatly stored in tackle boxes and storage bins from one end of the boat to another.

Clothing is essential. Rain gear is a must, and not the plastic poncho you can pick up for three bucks either. You will need stout rain suits that cost hundreds of dollars and are capable of standing up to the seventy miles per hour wind you will create for yourself at every tournament while running to your spot. Tournament shirts laced with the logos of all of your sponsors are required even if, early on in your career, most of them paid you with samples of their product that are not legal currency for any debts, public or private. Try as you may, the guy at the Arby's drive-thru just won't take a bag of plastic worms for an order of potato cakes. In a weird sort of chicken and egg thing, sponsors of bass fisherman rarely will pay actual money to an angler prior to that angler becoming successful on the tournament trail. Granted, sponsorship deals can be lucrative once an angler reaches the lofty heights of tournament success. These deals can easily reach the low six figures, but a guy could be emaciated by the sport well before this ever happens.

So it was that this was Clay's chosen career path. In the immediate, he had some decisions to make. Most notably, he had to decide which tournament trail he wanted to fish, BASS or FLW. Clay chose BASS. The BASS tour is the older of the two, the granddaddy of competitive bass fishing. Founded by Ray Scott, BASS was at one time the clear leader in the sport, but that can be argued today. At the time Clay decided to become a pro, most anglers that wanted to be professionals were signed up for BASS events at several different levels. Apparently, all Ford trucks built between 1980 and 1987 that were shipped to any dealer south of the Mason-Dixon line came with a BASS member sticker on the back window as standard equipment, a fact that remains unchecked for validity but sounds reasonable enough. Scott managed to turn his business idea for competitive fishing, also known as the "brain storm in a rain storm," into quite a successful endeavor. At its peak, BASS had 600,000 dues paying members. Scott once remarked that every time a new member joined, he would feel a lump in his pocketbook.

Clay started his career at the very bottom of the ladder, a level called the Federation. The Federation is the hard-core group of anglers that make the sport successful, the weekend anglers that spend most of the money on the products and most of the time keeping the resource viable through volunteer habitat work. Today, both the FLW and BASS organizations have a version of this important group of anglers. Although most of the fishermen at this level do not aspire to be professionals, many of them could beat the top pros on any given day in a winner take all single day event. Keeping the streak alive over an entire season would be difficult. However, a majority of those same top ranked pros would probably debate even this small bone being thrown to the amateurs, if given the chance. Certainly they are free to write their own books on this subject, but since they have not written this one, the point is ours for now.

Clay would fish the Alabama BASS Federation trail to gain valuable experience as he worked to move up to the next level in BASS, the Invitational tour.

*****

Clay figured correctly that the Federation level would allow him to sharpen the skills that separate the winners from the losers in a tournament. The truth of the matter is that when the bite is wide open anyone can catch fish, and these horse races can be won by anyone lucky enough to get the biggest bites, but the art of fishing, the skill, comes when the bite is tough. Certain anglers can scratch fish out of almost any situation that presents itself. If there is one single attribute, separating the consistent winners from the consistent losers, it is this ability to conjure fish when none seem to be around. All of the anglers that can do this are students of the environment, keen observers of the clues that Mother Nature provides to them.

Bass fishing has some inherent differences from other sports. First, the playing field can be tens of thousands of acres and the fish always have the home field advantage. Thrown in the mix is the fact that the opponent is not even human. You can't do anything to get inside the head of a bass. There is no way to intimidate a fish. You can intimidate your fellow competitors- some anglers are masters of this technique- but the fish remain immune to any of it. Bass fishing is an all weather sport. The only time a tournament is suspended is in rare cases of lightning or particularly heavy wind. For the most part, you play in whatever weather is on hand at the time, freezing cold or boiling hot are not exempt. This presented a problem for Clay. Because of his small size, Clay is not capable of sweating enough to stay cool or circulating enough blood to stay warm. Because the show must go on regardless of the weather, Clay would need to develop a plan to protect himself from the elements as much as possible.

Beyond that, Clay needed to develop a tournament plan for each event. Anglers use their practice to produce a game plan for the tournament itself. The plan has to take account of conditions that can change rapidly during the event. Weather patterns can fluctuate. Previously productive water can become non-productive due to the natural movement of fish around the area. Other anglers can crowd your spot, making your plan less effective or forcing you to move to another spot you identified in practice. Techniques need to be identified that produce reaction or forage bites, decisions made about proper lure selection, colors and presentations.

Clay needed to develop more practical plans also, a road map that allowed him to do things in ways that were different from the other anglers. For instance, how would Clay tie and retie his lures quickly? Bass anglers change lures frequently, sometimes several times in succession. Clay ties his lures to the line using his mouth. Prior to fishing for money, he would need to become extremely proficient at doing this. Through trial and error he determined the fastest way to make a lure change- sticking the hooks of the lure in his stump, cutting the lure off with his teeth, and retying it with his tongue. Perhaps you have been to several county fairs and watched many goat roping contests in your life, but it is guaranteed that you have never seen anything quite like this.

Clay also needed to refine his casting. The best anglers in the world can knock the silly grin off your face with a jig from fifty feet away. Bass are exceedingly structure conscience. They generally utilize cover to ambush unsuspecting prey as it swims by. Because they tend to be an apex predator in most places, they are somewhat lazy and will simply wait for the next poor soul that comes along if the choice before them is too far away or requires too much effort to go and get. Due to this fact, casting becomes a game of inches. The difference between a good cast and a poor cast can be no more than the difference between Candidate A and Candidate B in most elections. However, in bass fishing the lesser of two evils seldom works like it does in politics and fish rarely feed on the same old party line.

The list of things Clay needed to master must have seemed endless. The bottom line is that all of the equipment he would be using- the boats and rods, reels and lures- all of it had been designed to be used by a person with arms and legs, hands and feet. Clay had none of those and was not going to strap on any fakes, either.

Clay would need hundreds of hours of trial by fire just to draw even to the starting line.

*****

Clarence began making phone calls to the Alabama Bass Federation to make certain that Clay would be allowed to fish. There was a good deal of initial skepticism from the other side of the table. Although Clay had fished in many local tournaments with Federation members, even some Dixie Bass events that are a notch up from the local derby trail, there were certain BASS rules that would need to be addressed. Foremost amongst these was a rule that all participants need to be capable of giving aid to another participant, especially aid to your partner if the partner ends up falling out of the boat. These are practical rules designed to promote safety, especially when water temperatures can creep down to the low forty-degree range at some events. The word capable, and how it applies to the participants, is open to interpretation. Bass anglers come in all sizes and shapes. A stringent physical conditioning program is noticeably missing from the daily routine of some of the anglers that regularly fish tournaments. A comprehensive audit of the over-all physical abilities of the standard pool of tournament anglers may disclose an alarming deficiency of what some would describe as at or near optimum height/ weight ratios. In some tournaments, there is even a rule

against taking your shirt off, and it's not there by accident. A guy is really left to wonder how many average anglers could help themselves back to the boat let alone their partner.

As anyone that bass fishes already knows, the rules are the rules. They are- more often than not- applied to all participants on an equal basis, at least at the entry level of the sport. So, Clay would have to prove himself capable of conforming to the requirements. An audition of sorts was arranged. Clay would participate in a Federation event paired as the partner of an official from the organization. On the day of the event, Clarence helped Clay get his tackle and rods organized in the boat and then waited for Clay and his partner to return at the end of the day. Clarence hoped for the best, but knew that there was little he could do to help Clay pass muster.

Finally, the pair arrived back at the dock. The Federation official walked up to Clarence who was waiting by the launch ramp. The official was short and to the point in his prognosis of Clay and his ability. "Clay," he said, "is more than capable of fishing whenever and wherever he wants to."

Only later did Clarence learn that Clay had beaten his partner soundly that day.

*****

Clay Dyer went on to fish several Federation events in 1996, bagging a top-fifty finish on his first try. He joined a local club that was aligned with the BASS Federation to gain priority entry in some events. He surrounded himself with other club members, and they would all talk about fishing for hours on end. Beverly and Clarence went with Clay to the tournaments to help with the logistics. Soon Clay was contending in most events and was a steady performer.

Along the way, he was also picking up the valuable experience he knew he would need later when he moved up to the Invitational tour. He became totally comfortable driving his boat in even the roughest water. Several times he drew a co-angler partner at a tournament that did not know him. Without the benefit of already knowing Clay, it can be a bit of a mental exercise to work through the fact that he will be operating the boat that you will be in the next day. Clay could sense the hesitation and never made the situation any better, preferring instead to tell a litany of stories about how he had lost his limbs one at a time in various boat wrecks over the years. Some fact checking may again be in order, but if general memory of earlier interviews stands correct, this is sometimes how it went. Whatever the case, it does remain an actual fact that Clay originally wanted to call this book, "Bass Fishing Has Already Cost Me Two Legs and an Arm" but that title was rejected early on in the process.

Clay fished well enough to qualify for the state championship in three of the six years that he fished the Federation. This is quite an achievement in a state that is known to have one of the best Federations in the country, featuring some of the best anglers at that level.

After fishing the Federation for over half a decade, Clay was qualified to move up the ladder. He also felt that he was ready to go higher in the sport. He had paid some dues and had been able to save some money for the higher fee trail he was moving to.

He had also attracted the notice of a sponsor, one that was willing to help support his growing need for entry fees and travel money. Dave Ittner is the Director of Marketing for Lowrance Electronics. Lowrance manufacturers the advanced electronics an angler uses to locate fish and navigate his surroundings. Ittner is in charge of a stable of high quality anglers that represent Lowrance products on the tours. Jay Yelas is there, Skeet Reese too, along with Ish Monroe and many others. Lowrance is one of those coveted sponsors that all the anglers want. The trouble is that Ittner runs an Augusta National style program. You don't ask to be a part of the team, Lowrance asks you. In this way, Bill Gates is not a member of the esteemed golf club and many of the world's best anglers don't have a Lowrance logo displayed on their tournament shirt.

Ittner saw Clay in 2002 at the Bassmaster Classic, the end of year championship for the top reaches of the BASS tour. Clay was there to enjoy the event as a fan and dream of the day he too would be fishing the event. Struck by his perseverance and ability to relate to people, and after a long meeting with him, Ittner asked Clay to join the Lowrance team. This is instructive as Ittner can choose from any angler he wants, yet he immediately saw what he needed in Clay.

So in short order, Clay had qualified to move up, had the desire and the means to do so, and was now one step away from the top level of the sport. Things were going his way in spades, and his hard work was paying off.

A short time later BASS declined to let him participate in the Invitational tour citing the same angler aid rule that was an issue earlier. There was no debate, no one to argue the point with. Clay would not be allowed to advance.

Six years of fishing gone in an instant.

From Left to Right:
nephew Pride Dyer, brother Chris and Clay

Clay on Rejection:

"I never made an issue of BASS not letting me advance to the Invitational tour. What would be the point in forcing someone to accept you? I just wanted to go where I would be accepted or not accepted on my own merits."

Starting Over

Needless to say, Clay was dejected and more than a little hurt that BASS, after all this time, would now exclude him based on interpretation of a rule he thought had been dealt with so long ago. His options were varied, but none of them was particularly interesting to him. Years before, BASS had been taken to court over the exclusion of women from BASS events. The arguments against women are weak by modern standards being based on petty issues like how anglers would relieve themselves during an event. BASS events were conducted on public waterways, and Federal law applied. Women were soon fishing BASS events, but the ones doing so felt anything but welcome, were often categorized as something they were not, and generally had a tough go of things. It's worth noting that now women can even have their own sanctioned tour under the BASS umbrella, the grinding gears of progress finally catching up to the modern, less Neanderthal era. The FLW tour has never had a restriction against women participating, perhaps because it's roots run a couple decades shallower than those of BASS.

It is not a question of what would have happened had Clay decided to pursue the matter further. The law is clear, and BASS would undoubtedly have had to provide the necessary accommodations to allow Clay to participate. However, Clay did not want an accommodation. He wanted to compete head-to-head with the other anglers without special disposition or what anyone could claim was an advantage due to his limitations. Clay was not qualified to fish the FLW tour at this point as he had not spent any time learning the ropes on that side of the ledger. By and large, FLW fished different tournament water than did BASS, and Clay was unfamiliar with most of those fisheries. FLW had a different set of sponsor logo rules, and all non-FLW sponsor logos were banned from the weigh-in stage and final tournament day. This made it difficult to get and keep sponsors as many companies in the industry view the return on angler sponsoring in FLW to be low-or even non-existent. The option was to catch on with an FLW sponsor team. Although the FLW constricts logo display from non-tour companies, they do, in a noteworthy difference from BASS, actively recruit and support anglers to fish on teams put together by FLW sponsors.

Again, the chicken and the egg that is common in bass

fishing sponsorships.

To get a spot on a team, you must be an accomplished FLW angler. To make it to that level, you are largely on your own, perhaps without much sponsor help at all, paying your own way as you go along. But a huge positive to Clay was that the FLW tour makes a claim to be family friendly. A claim that they back up with action in several ways. Foremost, FLW does not accept alcohol or tobacco sponsors. BASS does, and the signing of Busch Beer to a sponsorship agreement in 2003 lead to any number of problems for BASS, including several name anglers deciding to decline participation.

This was attractive at some levels to Clay, because he thought that he would have a better message to promote to others if the tour he fished was naturally skewed toward more traditional values. Still the problem remained, he was not qualified to fish the tour and would need to start over.

Clay retracted his fishing back to the local derby and jackpot events he had started in years before. Once more he started climbing the ladder. This time his eye was on a new tour, the FLW Everstart, the mid-level tour stop that leads to the highest reaches of the FLW organization, the FLW Tour. It would be two years before he would fish his first Everstart event. Two years of keeping his skills up and searching for additional sponsors to help him along the way. Lowrance stuck with Clay during this time, as did Strike King and Minnkota. These three sponsors would form the core of companies that would help push him, eventually, to the next level.

*****

It was also during this time that Clay began to put together a short presentation about his life and his fishing. In what would become his personal testimony, he started to piece together a message that he thought he could deliver to church groups. A message that would reach out to people, especially kids, and give them a glimpse of the source of his optimism. It occurred to Clay that maybe this was the way to reach people, a way to connect with them. He hoped that people would look at him and realize that God gives certain gifts to all of us although these gifts rarely look the same from person to person. The more important piece of the puzzle is how you choose to use those gifts. Would you put them to good use, or would you prefer to let them sleep? Whatever the case, it was becoming clear to Clay that his fishing was to be used as the vehicle to reach people with his message of hope. Clay reasoned that if anyone had a reason to give up, it was him. The fact that God would not let him was an important piece of news, because it also meant that if you put in the time, God will help you put your skills to work as well.

Clay took the entire 2002 and 2003 seasons off from any national tour. He and Clarence fished some local events, and Beverly and Clay fished still others. Clarence was amazed at Clay's skills as an angler and figured that the plan to turn professional just might work. In 2004, Clay made the transition to the Everstart FLW tour.

Soon after signing up to fish his first FLW event, Clay

received a call from the FLW office. Coming to the phone, he remembers thinking that this would be a repeat of the disaster earlier with BASS. FLW had combed the rules and found some way to keep him from competing. Perhaps some other angler had made a flap about things, that certainly is never out of the question when it comes to these matters. Clay had made the Everstart with the support of Stratos, the boat manufacturer he was aligned with. Maybe some other Stratos pro-staffer had claimed his spot? Could it be that, again just on the brink of realizing his dream, he would be denied the opportunity based on some "out" the tour had found?

Coming to the phone, all of this was going through Clay's mind. He wasn't sure he could be as gracious about being snubbed as he was the last time. Clay picked up the receiver. On the other end was Chris Jones, the FLW employee in charge of the Everstart tour.

"Welcome to FLW," Chris said. "Is there anything we can do for you?"

Finally, Clay had been accepted to fish a tour that had a clearly defined route to the top of the sport. There were no restrictions placed on him, no need to prove that he had what it took before being allowed to participate. He would go out on the tour and face the other anglers square up. Some of these anglers would qualify to advance further in the sport while the majority would not. Some would flame out, unable to perform well enough to cover their costs, and be gone after only a few events. But for the anglers that could fish well enough to advance, the big show was right there in front of them, waiting for them to prove themselves. Clay intended to be one of those anglers.

Anglers advance in bass fishing based on points accumulated during a season. These points are distributed via the individual results of each event. The higher the finish, the more points are accrued. At the end of the year, the points determine the Angler of the Year as well as which anglers are invited to fish the next level, as well as any season ending championship or other special event. During an event, and as the events gel together to form a season, anglers are faced with a strategy decision: should they fish to win or fish for points? Most professional anglers will tell you they fish to win, but a statistical analysis of the field suggests something different altogether. The fact that it often is said that the majority of the same anglers would rather win Angler of the Year than the year-end championship is telling. The Catch-22 is that many times an angler must take a significant risk to actually win an event. This "swinging for the fences" can work to an angler's advantage when it pans out but may also exclude simply hitting a solid double and moving up in the standings.

Clay decided to make steady progress and the accumulation of points the primary goal of his rookie season. Certainly, he would like to make a final day cut and eventually win an event. These are goals he talks about freely. As Jay Yelas points out in the ESPN special segment discussed earlier, the day Clay does so will bring the house down. On several occasions during the 2004 and 2005

Everstart season, Clay came close to making the finals, fishing well in the first and second days of competition. The hump was elusive, however, and he did not ever quite climb the final few feet and make the exclusion round. He accumulated enough points to advance to the FLW Series. The FLW Series is a new tour developed by the FLW primarily to accommodate several top BASS anglers that chose not to participate in the BASS Elite series and the $55,000 in entry fees that come with it. Clay had now made the highest level of fishing, at least from a practical perspective. There are arguments both for and against any tour, the debate about which tour is truly the best goes on ad infinitum. Certainly the BASS Elite tour can claim supremacy from the standpoint of difficulty related to earning a qualification. The FLW Tour is no slouch either, featuring events that have as much glitz and glamour as anything BASS produces with the possible exception of the Bassmaster Classic, the granddaddy of all the year end championships. The FLW Series is slotted somewhere in the ballpark also, featuring tough competition from seasoned veterans of the sport as well. Among the three, about 600 of the 35 million bass fisherman in the U.S. participate so you can do your own math.

Wherever you come down on the "which is better than which" debate, as an angler you have about a one in sixty thousand chance of ever seeing your name on the active duty roster in any of them.

If you are Clay Dyer, you can take a great degree of pride in the fact that you are the first, and most likely the

last, head and torso only combination to reach the bright
lights in the sport.

Clay on No Limbs:

"I think it's very cool. I love being like I am. It has given me the opportunity to do things, experience things, and share things I probably never would have otherwise."

Running with the Big Dogs

Clay would fish selected FLW Tour events in 2006, as well as continue fishing the Everstart series, which had now been renamed the Stren series. The Stren series would allow Clay to fish tournaments that were closer to home while allowing the chance to make some extra money. The estimated cost of fishing an entire season on the FLW Tour works out to be about $60,000. This includes entry fees as well as travel expenses. In Clay's case his, expenses also include a traveling partner, someone to go with him to the events as his driver and helper in the mornings and evenings. Beverly and Clarence would provide this important function when they were able, but fishing was now a more than fulltime job for Clay and neither parent could miss an unreasonable amount of work.

Clay with the #1 ranked angler in the world, Kevin VanDam

Clay with George Cochran

Clay with Jimmy Houston

To make all of this a reality, Clay needed an extra sponsor or two. BassFan (the industry leader in on-line bass fishing news reporting) was added as a sponsor in early 2006. Clay would represent the entirety of the BassFan Pro Team at the FLW Tour level. He would run a BassFan.com wrapped tour boat. Unfortunately for Clay, the BassFan brand color palette is identical to the team colors of one Auburn University. Clay would have to hide the boat in a brush pile while at home to keep himself from learning the true meaning of a Crimson Tide, said lesson coming from his own mother. Strike King also upped their ante with Clay, their corporate colors leaning more toward the University of Nevada, hence no threat to anyone's personal safety in the greater North Alabama area. It should be noted that during this time, when Clay was struggling with his new Auburn colored boat, a tragedy of sorts took place. During a particularly cold night the Ralph Brown Draughon Library at Auburn University burned down. It burned up both the books, and one of them was not even colored in yet. That's a good joke and you can have it as a bonus, no extra cost. Feel free to insert whatever college or university name you want in the set-up line.

Clay also began to work with Elvin Smith. Smith is a Dallas Patent Attorney turned professional angler business manager. In some circles, he would be called an agent but the word went out long ago from some of the sport's power brokers that agents are not welcome in bass fishing. Elvin has a stable of top end anglers that he does provide management of contracts and personal representation to, but does not agent for.

Elvin began working with Clay to sharpen his presentation and his personal testimony. Based on the word DREAM as an acronym, Clay and Elvin shaped a message that describes how Clay is "living the dream," with each letter in the word standing in for words like Determination, Resources and on down the line to Motivation. He developed a web presence for Clay so that people can keep up with his progress on the tour. Most importantly, Elvin began promoting Clay as a speaker to churches and business organizations. This second prong of Clay's career appealed to Clay, because it allowed him to carry his message to audiences nationwide, keeping his half of the deal that had been put in front of him long ago at the youth rally. Clay began to routinely address groups, and his optimism and pride in place is contagious to most, earning him high praise as a speaker and motivator.

As the season progressed, Clay maintained his qualification and came close to his goal of making a final. He fished well enough to start to be a threat, and people began to wonder when he would break out, when they would see him in the winner's circle.

*****

At this writing Clay continues both with his fishing and his public speaking, donating fifteen percent of his sponsor income to causes that benefit children and the disabled. Included here is Cast for Kids, a Seattle based

organization that takes special needs kids fishing and utilizes Clay as their national spokesman.

While it is impossible for anyone following God's plan to know the future in any exact sense, Clay plans to continue with both endeavors. Making the final day cut is still the elephant in the room for Clay, but, with any luck at all, he should have a freezer full of elephant fillets sometime in the 2008 season.

The word "can't" still is not found anywhere in the Clay Dyer dictionary.

Obviously not the same elephant.

Clay on Life:

"Some ask whether the glass is half full or half empty. I don't think it matters much. I just try to make the best use out of what's there."

Clay's response to his dad's question at birth?

"The view from down here is just fine."

If you want to learn more about Clay,
please visit his website at:

www.claydyerfishing.com

Join Clay's fan club at:

www.teamdyer.com

DIVISION C WINNERS

(From left) third place, John Mills; second, Clay Dyar; and first, David Corbitt.